The Us
Abuse of Drugs

A Christian Response

Luke Bretherton

Lecturer in Theology and Ministry
King's College, London

GROVE BOOKS LIMITED
RIDLEY HALL RD CAMBRIDGE CB3 9HU

Contents

First Impression July 2004
ISSN 1470-854X
ISBN 1 85174 566 1

Introduction 1

There is a growing body of literature that discusses drug use and the problems associated with it. Some of this literature has what might be called a 'spiritual' dimension: that is, it incorporates some discussion of the religious uses of and ideas about drugs. However, given the prevalence of drug use, both today and in ages past, there is remarkably little written about drugs from a Christian theological perspective. This booklet is a small step in redressing this lacuna in theological reflection.

The booklet aims to identify the moral problems that underlie contemporary patterns of drug use and to contrast a theological assessment of these problems with other approaches to analysing and responding to the use and abuse of drugs. In doing so, it will seek to integrate cultural analysis, pastoral care, spirituality, doctrine and ethics, viewing each of these supposedly discrete fields as central to forming a coherent response to the issue.

What will not be considered are arguments for or against the legalization of any particular drug. The bracketing of the question of legality is necessary in order to address the theological and moral issues relating to drugs on their own terms. This is not to say that questions about the legalization or otherwise of drugs are unimportant, it is simply that questions regarding law and social policy are not the focus of this booklet.

My primary thesis is that modern patterns of legal and illegal drug use are:

- a paradigmatic instance of the technocratic conception of the body as an object of manipulation, subject to a regime of hyper-control;
- the fruit of contemporary patterns of mass consumption; and
- in what they say about the human body and the way they shape human life together, contemporary patterns of drug use contrast sharply with a theological account of the place of drugs in human life.

I will argue that drugs culture cannot be separated off as a dark realm, removed from everyday life. Rather, insofar as such a thing can be identified, it is a microcosm of, and intrinsically woven into, the mainstream of contemporary culture. By addressing the use and abuse of drugs in a broad frame of reference I hope to open up new perspectives on drugs that fund constructive and life-bringing ways of addressing the problems associated with drug use in all its aspects.

2   The Scope of the Problem

The use and abuse of drugs affects every realm of life.

Concerns around abuse have led to the introduction of drug testing in many companies and in many sports. At the same time behavioural problems are increasingly being medicalized with large numbers of children on drugs such as Ritalin. The use of drugs is central to many of the most pressing international issues that confront us today and includes:

- dealing with the AIDS pandemic;
- the regulation of international markets and the problem of money laundering;
- the 'war on terror';[1] and
- the debate on the environment.[2]

There are periodic calls for the legalization of drugs such as cannabis at the same time as ongoing debates about how to tackle the link between crime and drug use. Alongside this, one of the ruling ideals of contemporary Western society—namely, that of 'health'—makes debates about the use of drugs in healthcare (notably, the issue of resource allocation in health care) and the classification and use of various alternative or complementary medicines a recurring theme in social and political discourse. In short, wherever we look, whether it be in the arena of work, recreation, domestic politics and social life or international relations, we find disputes about the use, abuse, production and distribution of drugs. Thus, before giving a formal definition of the term 'drug' it is important to identify the true scope of the problem.

Contemporary Contradictions

Contemporary attitudes to drug use are contradictory. On the one hand, we see drugs as a good thing, providing relief from suffering and enabling us to improve the functioning of our bodies. On the other, drugs are seen to destabilize the 'normal' functioning of society and individuals. For example, those drugs classed as illegal are often perceived as undermining the civil, social and economic order of society and this threat justifies in turn huge military expenditure in the 'war on drugs.' At the same time, ever more 'medicinal' drugs are being manufactured in order to help us lead healthier and happier lives, for example, the use of appetite suppressants to control obesity. But at the same time, the health benefits of other drugs are being called into question— it is now suggested that the negative impact of hormone replacement therapy outweighs its therapeutic value. This contradiction can be seen most clearly in the historical development of contemporary patterns of drug use.

The systematic collation of knowledge about plants and their effects on the human body has ancient roots

All cultures throughout history have used plants for a variety of therapeutic and religious purposes. The systematic collation of knowledge about plants and their effects on the human body has ancient roots. For example, one of the oldest systems of medicine is the Ayurvedic system originating in India around 3,000 years ago. Another ancient use of plants is the utilization of their psychoactive properties—either direct (as with coca or cannabis) or indirect (as with alcohol derived from fermented grapes)—to cope with the toil, physical pain and stresses of everyday working life and to act as a focal point for social interaction. However, drug use, as practised today is coextensive with the development and intensification of certain, central features of modernity.

Drugs and Modernity

Contemporary patterns of drug use cannot be understood outside of their relationship to the development of technology (notably chemical technology), of global trade (initially through colonialism), of industrialization and mass consumerism, and of bureaucratic control and the expansion of the nation-state.[3] For example, the introduction, into early modern Europe, of coffee and tea, the most commonly used drugs, was inextricably bound up with the growth of colonialization and the beginnings of mass consumption.[4] Likewise, cannabis, largely unknown in Europe before the eighteenth century, was introduced into Europe through colonial expansion into Algeria, Egypt and India.[5] Alongside the increasing range of plants available for use from the early modern period onwards was the application of the scientific method to medical practice and the study of plants. This application led to the isolation of alkaloids and the creation of synthetic and semi-synthetic drugs for medicinal use. Such developments were then combined with industrialized means of production. For example, cocaine, the psychoactive alkaloid in coca leaves, was identified in 1860 and its industrial production was begun in 1862.[6]

The introduction of cannabis into Europe provides a case study in the pattern of this expansion. The effects of cannabis were known about in Europe from the eighteenth century onwards as a result of French and British colonial expansion and trade. Introduction was followed by a period of medical and recreational experimentation. Dr William Brooke O'Shaughnessy first began medical experiments with cannabis in the 1830s while around the same time Parisian bohemians, such as Flaubert, were experimenting with its more hedonistic potential. This experimentation led to its commercial exploitation. Under O'Shaughnessy's direction, a London pharmacist, Peter Squire, developed an extract and tincture of cannabis.[7] By 1887 cannabis cigarettes were sold by pharmacists for the 'immediate relief in all cases of Asthma, Nervous Coughs, Hoarseness, Loss of Voice, Facial Neuralgia and Sleeplessness.'[8] Inevitably, much of its use was not directly therapeutic. Concern about the effects of its use, both in Europe and its colonies, led to campaigns for greater restrictions on its use and control over its production. Official investigations were established in order to respond to the concerns being raised. For example, in 1893, the *Indian Hemp Drug Commission* was established to investigate the impact of the drug in India. From World War I onwards a policy of prohibition and severely restricted control was introduced. Similar patterns of introduction and experimentation, commercialization, taxation and/or legal regulation can be traced for virtually all other drugs.

From Taxation to Prohibition

Attitudes towards psychotropic drugs such as cannabis or opium underwent a marked shift from the end of the nineteenth century onwards. In general terms, the shift was marked by a change from taxation to prohibition and the criminalization of their use and distribution. This shift had a variety of causes:

- geo-political shifts, notably the rise of America as a world power and shifts in British Imperial policy;[9]

- economic developments, particularly what was needed from workers within industrial processes of production as against what was required of an agricultural labourer;

- social anxieties about how drug use sapped the fitness of a country for war (related to this were racist fears about 'foreigners' corrupting young people);

- greater understanding of the toxic and habit-forming properties of drugs resulting from scientific research;

- and the campaigns by Evangelicals, Socialists and other social reformers who were concerned about how drug use was morally corrosive and a pauperizer.

From these anxieties about what are now socially and politically proscribed drugs, as well as more general issues about drugs *per se*, five major areas of concern about the use and abuse of all drugs can be identified:

i   *Health and Safety* This includes effectiveness of drugs in dealing with perceived medical problems as well as the ways in which drugs are seen to militate against the promotion of health.

ii *Law and Order* This includes the legal regulation and bureaucratic administration and taxation of all drugs and the ways in which the misuse of drugs is linked to crime and social and personal disorder.

iii *Economic* The use of drugs has always been linked with patterns of trade and commerce, however, drug use and its social consequences are at the same time seen as a threat to economic prosperity, either at an individual or societal level.

iv *Technological* While linked with concerns around health and safety, a distinct area of concern is with the effectiveness of drugs to fulfil the tasks (medicinal or otherwise) they are produced for. This is illustrated by the development of pharmacogenomics which seeks to tailor drug treatment to individual needs and genetic make-up. These are being developed in response to the recognition that the same drug may have different effects on different sections of the population. For example, women may have a different level of response to a particular drug than men.

v   *Enhancement* Concern, both positive and negative, in relation to how drugs may enhance or amplify innate human capabilities. An example of what was seen as their positive function was the use of amphetamines to enable soldiers to fight for longer in World War II and the Vietnam War. The negative aspect of this concern has been most clearly articulated in relation to sport and how the use of steroids or other drugs enhance an athlete's abilities so as to give them an unfair advantage over other competitors.

We might also include under the heading of enhancement a subcategory of *connoisseurship*: this would include how some drugs can be aesthetically appreciated in their own right (such as wine), and give rise to a distinct tradition of appreciation and production (viticulture), and how certain drugs enhance the pleasure derived from other human activities (such as sexual intercourse or dancing).

Each of these categories has a moral dimension. However, apart from specifically theological concerns about certain kinds of drug use (for example, that drinking alcohol is 'unbiblical'), it is very hard to identify exactly what the moral problem is in relation to drug use *per se* (as distinct from more general concerns about lack of virtue and immorality of which drug use is a symptom) that social reformers have been concerned about. Most concern about drugs has been couched in one or other of the five categories listed above, but these ways of framing the use and abuse of drugs fail to address the real *moral* dimensions of drug use. Health and safety concerns about the use of drugs come close, but such concerns are still essentially functional. The legal, economic and technological concerns about drug use are more procedural concerns than moral ones. The concern is not whether taking any particular drug is moral or immoral, right or wrong, but what constitutes the best way to manage and regulate the use, distribution and production of a drug. However, one concern, that of the use of drugs in sport to gain an advantage over other competitors, is, perhaps, the most morally insightful concern because it raises the issue of justice, that is, whether enhancing one's sporting abilities through drugs fair or unfair. Behind this question of justice is the more difficult question of what the limits and proper uses of the human body are—in this case, in relation to sport. This is the underlying moral question we must address if we are to assess what a Christian response to the use and abuse of drugs should be. It is the underlying moral question because discerning what bodies are for is crucial to determining whether any particular drug enables or disables the proper ends or *telos* of the body and thus what the limits to its uses are and at what point use has become abuse. But before we do this, we must be clear what the term 'drug' means.

The legal, economic and technological concerns about drug use are more procedural concerns than moral concerns

Defining Terms 3

What are we talking about when we talk about drugs?

The World Health Organization defines a 'drug' as 'any substance that, when taken into the living organism, may modify one or more of its functions.' This definition attempts to define the term 'drug' neutrally. A more colloquial usage is less broad than the WHO definition and uses the term 'drugs' to refer to currently illicit drugs such as cannabis or cocaine. This colloquial usage points to only one, negative aspect of drug use. But when defining the term 'drugs' we must take into account all aspects of the term. Yet this itself is problematic.

> *When defining the term 'drugs' we must take into account all aspects of the term*

Drugs are a deeply ambiguous phenomenon. Their ambiguity lies in the difficulty we have in discerning how far their goodness is poisoning the user or the poisonous aspects of a drug are being used to good effect. For example, heroin is both a poison and a medicine and acts as both a poison and a pain relief simultaneously. Thus, we must heed the musings of the Friar in *Romeo and Juliet* (a play in which the dramatic device turns on the ambiguous nature of a drug) when he states:

> Within the infant rind of this weak flower
> Poison hath residence, and medicine power
> (*Romeo and Juliet*, II.iii.23–30)

Our efforts to understand the use and abuse of drugs will prove futile if we try falsely to resolve the ambiguity of the human relationship with drugs by either emphasizing one aspect (they are bad/they are good) or by claiming drugs are neutral. Drugs are never neutral: they have concrete effects upon us, effects which may promote or diminish human flourishing or do both simultaneously. The question before us is: how do we cope with this ambiguity?

> *The question before us is: how do we cope with this ambiguity?*

There is a further problem that attends defining the term drug. The use and abuse of drugs is a highly contentious issue and drugs and drug users have often served as scapegoats in contemporary culture.[10] In analysing drug use, we must beware the moral panics and alarmist accounts that have attended most drugs from coffee to crack cocaine.[11] For example, John Wesley inveighed against tea for its allegedly effeminate aura and for the way it inculcated indolence.[12] We must also avoid the tendency to scapegoat drugs users or any particular section of society, including doctors, pharmaceutical companies, or 'drug barons' for the problems drugs can cause. Likewise, we must not imbue drugs themselves with a malevolent agency. When 'drugs' become an omnipotent demon with the power to curtail free will and drag the unsuspecting victim into 'addiction,' crime, and death, it becomes rational to 'wage war' on the demon, a war which can come to justify any measure, whatever its ecological, human or economic cost.[13] Thus, when thinking about drugs we must take account of their ambiguity and avoid either scapegoating one section of society (*eg* drug barons, drug users etc) or imbuing drugs themselves with a demonic agency. Both of these approaches are simplistic and mask the real nature of the problem.

> *We must not imbue drugs themselves with a malevolent agency*

Bearing all this in mind, the term 'drugs' can be defined heuristically as referring to *chemical substances that when taken into the human body, through ingestion, injection or some other means, modifies one or more of the capacities of the body for either ampliative or therapeutic purposes and not for feeding or nourishing the body.*[14]

Let me explain. Drugs are distinguished from a warm pair of shoes in that the bodily changes they effect are accomplished through becoming part of the body's chemistry rather than external stimulation. For example, in contrast to the actions of a pumice stone, a non-cosmetic skin cream, such as an eczema cream, works through being absorbed into the body. Drugs are also to be distinguished from changes brought about by ascetic practices (for example, fasting) in that drugs are an external substance added to the body rather than simply a somatic or bodily exercise. Furthermore, although certain substances may also be used as food, such use is distinct from their use as a drug, although the use of a chemical substance as a drug and as physical nourishment may be simultaneous, as with drinking beer. Most importantly, the use of a substance as a drug is identified by particular kinds of usage:

i *Ampliative drug use* that seeks to augment or enhance an inherent capacity of the body for technical, recreational or religious purposes. Ampliative drug use ranges from steroids that enhance muscle performance to alcohol that enables conviviality. Such use might or might not be 'good' depending on the particular end or goal such enhancement seeks.[15]

ii **Therapeutic drug use** that seeks to cure or prevent or fix a real or perceived ailment of the body. Therapeutic drug use ranges from using antibiotics to prevent or heal an infection to using morphine as an analgesic. Again, there can be therapeutic use and misuse of drugs, such as over-prescription of antibiotics leading to new strains of super-bacteria.

So when we are discussing drugs we need to be careful about what we mean by the term. We also need to be careful about who we identify as drug users. We live in a drug culture. All of us make constant use of drugs, and drug use is a central feature of modern Western patterns of life.

4

Drugs and the Chemical Generation

So why are drugs such a central feature of contemporary Western culture? There seem to be three basic reasons.

> i We live in a technological culture which seeks to shape and manipulate the human body through technology, and drugs are a major means for doing this.
>
> ii We live in a culture that seeks to avoid pain and maintain a certain comfort level. Again, drugs are a major way to achieve this.
>
> iii We live in a consumer culture and drugs—illegal or legal—are an important consumer product.

Let me expand on each of these in turn.

Drugs as a Symptom of a Technocratic Culture

Drugs—as a technology—are central to Western society, and the way we approach drugs is characterized by seeing them as a means by which to manipulate and exploit our bodies according to our will and as an expression of our 'freedom.'

The environment and the human body have become raw material for manipulation and shaping according to our will

We live in an age when the environment and the human body are no longer seen as having given ends or goals which we may discern and judge how best to fulfil. Instead, they have become raw material for manipulation and shaping according to our will or choice. We have lost the ability to discern whether technical intervention is appropriate or not because everything is seen as a resource waiting to be exploited. However, unless we are attentive to creation and shape our own constructions in response to it, creation—whether it be the climate, the Amazonian rain-forests or our bodies—will break down. Thus the paradox of modern culture is that by asserting our freedom over and against creation we end up hurting ourselves.[16]

This is exactly what happens with drugs. They are a technology we use to manipulate and control the body yet they have become a major social problem. I am not just referring to issues around crime and individual dependency. Society as a whole has become entirely dependent on drugs to maintain a particular conception and experience of normality characterized by comfort or what in German is called *gemütlichkeit*. We deploy lorry loads of syrups, pills, and lotions in order to liberate ourselves from the everyday tyranny of the body's aches, pains, tiredness, allergies and the general affects of ageing. And we are increasingly employing yet more kinds of drugs to tailor our personality and physical abilities to fulfil our desires or alleviate our anxieties about our sense of who we should be or what we should be able to achieve. One recent example of such tailoring is use of the drug Prozac. The psychologist Peter Kramer calls such tailoring 'cosmetic pharmacology.'[17] Yet, as with all human attempts at self-salvation from the effects of sin and death, the irony is that our liberation turns out to be bondage. We are, in effect, dependent on the technology of drugs to maintain our freedom from bodily necessity and constraint, but by constantly manipulating our body to maintain our cosiness, or to fulfil our desire to be a different kind of person, we find ourselves in self-contradiction. We require ever higher doses to circumvent the diminishing returns of the potions we use, we then require more treatments to heal us from the sickness these drugs induce, and ultimately, despite all our best efforts and the strictness of our regimes, we can never win the battle against a body in which death is at work (2 Cor 4.12). Ivan Illich identified the counterproductive dynamic at work in our technological, medicalized drugs culture as clinical, social and cultural 'iatrogenesis.' Drugs and medicine have themselves become a major threat to health.[18]

We are dependent on the technology of drugs to maintain our freedom from bodily necessity and constraint

Drugs as a Symptom of a Comfort-Seeking, Pain-Avoiding Culture

Central to the drive to maintain physical comfort and to be, in the words of Carl Elliot, 'better than well,' is the modern conception of suffering.[19] Within modernity illness, pain and suffering are pointless—they can play no role in helping us live our lives well. Suffering has become unintelligible in contemporary society. Suffering in any form must be eliminated through technical means. Thus, when all other drugs or bodily regimes of control fail, we are given another pill—Valium or Prozac—to make us feel happy or help us cope with our condition. However, the drive to maintain physical comfort, or, as is increasingly the case, to maintain a sense of self-fulfilment, ignores how physical or psychological pain is part of the way in which we may order our lives properly in response to the created order. For example, if I am tired and have a headache the body does not need a coffee and an aspirin, but a rest. Yet, under the logic of contemporary modern life, bodily pain does not serve to alert me to my social, economic or political conditions, so that I might ask, for instance, why I am having to work late. Rather, bodily pain is a provocation to tighten up my regime of control 'over' the body (I need to exercise more, eat better, buy a more comfortable chair or a stronger brand of headache pill and so on), and thus treat the body as an object of manipulation. The same can be said of the use of enhancement technologies to address psychological or emotional pain. The quest to change my body, whether pharmacologically or through surgery, to make me feel better about myself, ignores the need to address a lack of virtue or character or the need for emotional healing. As Illich argues, within our technological civilization, pain has become a demand 'for more drugs, hospitals, medical services, and other outputs of corporate impersonal care' and has become a source of 'political support for further corporate growth no matter what its human, social, or economic cost.'[20]

Much of the rhetoric that surrounds use of these drugs is of liberation— 'free your mind'

We see the same dynamic when it comes to recreational use of drugs like LSD, cannabis and ecstasy. Much of the rhetoric that surrounds use of these drugs is of liberation—'free your mind.' They are seen also as ampoules of rebellion and social non-conformity— 'turn on, tune in, drop out.'[21] Yet, such use is in actuality conformity to the heart of the modern project. The ways in which drugs such as cocaine are used reflects the desire to engineer an experience. Why risk not enjoying yourself when you can chemically ensure that you will like your friends, appreciate the music and will not get tired after a stressful week at work?

Far from freeing their minds, most clubbers are bureaucrats of fun

Yet such engineering or technological manipulation of experience imperils what it means to be human, for it deprives human existence itself of certain spontaneities of being and doing which depend upon the reality of a world which we have not made or imagined, but which simply confronts us to evoke our fear, love, and delight. A personal, spontaneous response to music and dancing are entirely different in kind from those resulting from a chemically manufactured one. Furthermore, drugs are used to manage the responses of the mind and body to maximize the enjoyment of a night out—Ecstasy (to make you happy), amphetamines or cocaine (to keep you going), LSD (for its visual effect) and cannabis or tamazepam (to chill out and 'come down' at the end of it all). And drug dealers are just another service industry, responding to consumer demand. Far from freeing their minds, most clubbers and weekend party animals are bureaucrats of fun, administrating their enjoyment like a corporate manager organizing his schedule.

> Beyond the rhetoric, taking drugs is deeply conformist and conservative: drug taking conforms to the technocratic logic of modernity and conserves those patterns of life that are shaped by a modern vision of the good life (whether hedonistic or otherwise). Taking drugs is thus a moral imperative within the logic of modernity: they are a valuable technology through which we can manage and manufacture a better, more fulfilling life.[22]

Drugs as a Symptom of a Consumer Culture

As well as being a symptom of a technocratic and pain-avoiding culture, our use of drugs is a symptom of consumerism. Unlike in previous eras, drugs are easily available items of mass production and consumption unmodulated by either time consuming, labour intensive processes (such as brewing), scarcity of resources, or socially constraining and disciplining practices such as ritualized religious consumption. Yet, there is more to drug use in a consumer culture than just the question of availability.

Why should our society be characterized as a consumer society?

What do I mean by the term consumerism? We cannot stay alive without consuming things and all societies—ancient and modern—have practised some form of conspicuous consumption, so why should our society be characterized as a consumer society?

Zygmunt Bauman argues that our society engages its members primarily in their capacity as consumers.[23] Bauman states: 'The way present-day society shapes up its members is dictated first and foremost by the need to play the role of the consumer, and the norm our society holds up to its members is that of the ability and willingness to play it.'[24] If we accept that our society is one in which the primary mode of involvement is as a consumer, rather than as an agriculturalist or warrior or hunter-gatherer, we must attend to how contemporary patterns of consumption shape the relationship between the body and drugs and encourage people to control their responses to life through adjusting their bodily chemistry.

We must consume things in order to live. However, as Robert Bocock comments: 'Consumption is founded on a *lack*—a desire always for something not there. Modern/postmodern consumers, therefore, will never be satisfied. The more they consume, the more they will desire to consume.'[25] He goes on to say: 'People living under the influence of postmodern capitalism's consumer culture will continue to desire the unattainable—that is the satiation of all their desires.'[26] Yet, one could go even further and suggest that what is important now is not the satiation of desire, but the desire of desire: that is, the need to have one's desire constantly stimulated in order to feel alive when life itself is conceived in terms of the need to consume more.

Within the context of a consumerist culture the human body has become one more object to be desired and consumed. We aspire to sculpt our bodies through exercise or modify them through surgery, we frame them through clothes in the best possible light, and buy food that will help us shape up in order to present our bodies as living sacrifices to a culture of conspicuous consumption. And drug use encapsulates a primary way in which we manipulate and maximize the hedonistic profitability of our bodies.

Drugs themselves—whether used for ampliative or therapeutic effect—are perhaps the ultimate consumer product. In a society in which, according to George Steiner's pithy aphorism, all cultural products are calculated for 'maximal impact and instant obsolescence,'[27] drugs give an instant, maximally intense hit and, unlike sunglasses or CDs, they are used up in one go.[28] Moreover, in a society of experience collectors, ampliative drug use bypasses the equipment and preparation needed for a parachute jump or sailing trip and do not require the spatial and temporal investment of an adventure holiday or visit to Disneyland; instead, they deliver a hit of pure experience without the need for training, travel or time. And apart from anything else there is a huge commercial investment in our continued use of drugs of all kinds.[29] In short, *in a consumer and capitalist society, it is entirely rational to take drugs for ampliative purposes.*[30] Drugs may poison and consume or use up our bodies, just as cars consume and use up our environment, but they powerfully satisfy and simultaneously foster the desire of persons whose bodies are conditioned and constantly aroused by consumer products lavishly displayed and advertised, and whose hearts and minds seek, above all else, the freedom to consume.

Summary

We can begin to see that to make sense of contemporary patterns of drug use we must situate drug use in a wider context and identify the underlying social, political and economic developments which shape our use of drugs. These developments have been identified as the technocratic, pain-avoiding and consumerist aspects of contemporary Western culture.

Drug Use Within Salvation History 5

Having analysed how contemporary patterns of drug use manifest particular features of modernity, I turn now to how drugs can be understood theologically within the history of redemption. It should be noted that the conclusions drawn from this theological account are not intended as ecclesiastical house rules but as having application beyond just the Christian community.

Drug Use in the Light of Creation

As stated before, drugs are ambiguous. All drugs, whether generated within creation (for example cannabis and opium) or fabricated from creation (for example, aspirin and MDMA) have the capacity to poison or heal, lead to human alienation or enable greater personal presence between humans.

The location of drug use is, in the first place, the human body, and the body is, in itself, a created good, with its own limits and purposes. Drug use should not usurp or overstep the created boundaries of the body. The use of drugs should instead seek to work within and attempt to fulfil the created goodness of the body. Thus, for example, the use of drugs to deny (rather than heal or enhance) the physical limits of the body, such as amphetamines to overcome or deny physical tiredness, are illicit because such use constitutes the claiming of an illegitimate freedom

Time and space are not constraints that we need liberation from

that is inherently self-defeating. For example, one of the limits a drug like amphetamines seeks to deny is the limit of time. Time and space are not constraints that we need liberation from. Human existence in time and space is not to be circumvented or diminished through technologies of perception. But as Christ's incarnation affirms, creation is the proper location for humans to live and work and have their being. Thus, physical time limits on the duration we can work are good in that they set boundaries that help shape and properly order human relations.

Perhaps the most important limit to the human body is that life itself has an end or goal beyond itself. Karl Barth states: 'Life is no second God, and therefore the respect due to it cannot rival the reverence owed to God.'[31] Barth points out that the respect owed to life as a good in itself has as its limitation

Christians seek to live within these limits, recognizing that between these limits lies the sphere of true freedom

'the will of God the Creator himself who commands it, and the horizon which is set for man by the same God with his determination for eternal life.'[32] What Barth says points to how Christians understand the basis of their life. It is not their own but received as a gift and loan from God which can only be fulfilled in communion with God. Thus Christians seek to live within these limits, recognizing that between these limits lies the sphere of true freedom. They bear their life in trust for a certain time and seek to discern how human life can respond appropriately to the good gift of creation and its inherent order. However, while life is a good, for Christians it is not the greatest good. The greatest good we seek is our eschatological communion with God and each other. When drugs are used to prolong, protect or fulfil (whether hedonistically or medically) life at any cost, then such use indicates that life itself has come to rival God in human estimation. In such cases drugs are being used illicitly; that is, they have become an adjunct to idolatry because they are being used to over-invest this present life with significance.

Drug Use in the Shadow of the Fall

That we live in need of redemption from our condition of slavery to sin and death has enormous ramifications for how drugs should be used. We cannot eliminate what causes us to stumble by banning or abstaining from drugs. Drugs may open a door to the sin of gluttony (for example, drunkenness) but drugs themselves are not the cause of such sin. Even those drugs that can induce a physiological dependency, for example heroin, may be used with temperance over long periods of time.[33] While exposure to a drug is a critical precondition to dependency or abuse, what leads to gluttony or dependency is the character and circumstances of a person rather than the substance itself.[34] Christ's teaching on what defiles us is an important check on over-investing drugs themselves with corrupting properties. Throughout the gospels Christ is portrayed as in conflict with many other programmes for the purification and holiness of Israel. One of the central conflicts is with an approach to holiness that involves ritual purity while ignoring character and intention. Mark 7.18–23 states:

> Jesus said to them, '...Do you not see that whatever goes into a person from outside cannot defile, since it enters not the heart but the stomach, and goes out into the sewer?' (Thus he declared all foods clean.) And he said, 'It is what comes out of a person that defiles. For it is from within, from the human heart, that evil intentions come:

> fornication, theft, murder, adultery, avarice, wickedness, deceit, licentiousness, envy, slander, pride, folly. All these evil things come from within, and they defile a person.'

The use of drugs may greatly exacerbate our folly and licentiousness, but drugs do not cause them. The contrast between Dr William Stewart Halsted and Samuel Taylor Coleridge illustrates how it is not drugs *per se* that lead to drug binges and the breakdown of an individual's personal life. Halsted (1852–1922), one of the four distinguished founders of the Johns Hopkins Medical School, sustained a dependency on morphine all his life while also being a practising surgeon of famed skill.[35] By comparison, Coleridge proved consistently unable to control his opium dependency and the effects of his physiological and psychological dependency on the drug greatly compounded his personal, artistic and professional problems. But the roots of Coleridge's problems lay not in his physiological dependency on opium but in tragic flaws in his character, for example, his procrastination.[36] If what causes problems with drugs is not initially or primarily the drugs themselves, but our sinful characters, then we must learn how to manage our responses to drugs in the light of our fallen condition. Managing our responses to drugs means undertaking to school the flesh and avoid establishing patterns of life (either corporately or individually) that encourage dependency on drugs. Thus, for example, to tackle illegal drug consumption effectively it may be wiser to invest in social policies that address consumerism rather than attempt prohibition.

It is important, at this point, to make a distinction between temperance and abstinence. Temperance movements have generally confused one with the other, but temperance does not mean abstinence. Rather, it means 'the practice or habit of exercising self-control or moderation.'[37] Temperance is thus what Paul is referring to with regard to sexual relations in 1 Thessalonians when he calls for each one of us to know 'how to control [our] own body in holiness and honour, not with lustful passion, like the Gentiles who do not know God' (1 Thess 4.3–5). John Paul II argues that the virtue of temperance is what Paul means when he calls for purity. In John Paul II's view the virtue of temperance has a twofold aspect. It is both abstention from the passion of lust and at the same time, control of one's own body in holiness and honour.[38] However, control and abstention from lust

Legalism and licence are two sides of the same coin

(rather than abstention from any particular created good) must be balanced with the need to avoid legalism. In Galatians 5 Paul talks of the mutual antipathy of Spirit and flesh (5.17). But as Oliver O'Donovan notes, Paul's use of the term flesh unites both flesh as 'desire' (*epithymia*) and flesh as 'law' (*nomos*).[39] In other words, legalism and licence are two sides of the same coin.

Thus, legalistic abstention from, and prohibition of, drugs is as pernicious as the gluttonous or lawless use of drugs. Both constitute a false valorization of one's own flesh and a denial of the work of the Spirit. Our proper response to drugs is one of temperate use, for it is through temperance that we properly respect the created goodness of the human body and grow in our detachment from what, in the human heart, is the fruit of the lusts of the flesh, rather than the fruit of the Holy Spirit.[40]

Affirming Creation and Avoiding Idolatry

We must also avoid over-investing any particular substance with demonic properties and denying the goodness of creation. Paul's teaching in 1Corinthians 8 is particularly relevant here. N T Wright sees 1 Corinthians 8 as an attempt to fight a battle on two fronts—against a Gnostic-like dualism (which constitutes the rejection of the goodness of the created order) and against paganism (which constitutes the deification of the created order).[41] Drugs can become a form of idolatry or be used, like meat, as part of a wider system of idolatry. We have already analysed the link between drugs and the idolatry of consumerism. Now for Paul, idols have no ontological existence (1 Cor 8.4) and the things we consume do not, in and of themselves, establish our relationship with God or alienate us from God (1 Cor 8.8). But idols, and meat sacrificed to them, signal a real phenomenon that must be dealt with and not sidestepped. To place oneself in the sphere of idols is to be involved in demon worship. Wright states that for Paul:

> To enter an idol's temple, and eat there alongside those who are actually intending to share fellowship with this non-god, this hand-made pseudo-god—this is to invite created powers to have an authority over one which they do not possess, a power which belongs only to the creator-God revealed in and through Jesus the Messiah.[42]

Therefore we may conclude that Paul is saying, avoid eating meat in temples of idolatry, but the purchase and consumption of meat from the market is licit (for to say anything else would be to lapse into a Gnostic denial of the goodness of creation).

Our problem, of course, is that the marketplace has become the temple. In this situation there must be an emphasis on creating mature habits of consumption, characterized by temperance, which are neither bound by the practices of the idolatry of consumerism, nor subject to the idolatry of technology, but directed to consummation in Christ. By saying that our primary concern is developing temperance in how we use drugs, am I saying that no drug is off limits? As with meat sacrificed to idols, so we must say of drugs:

'"All things are lawful," but not all things are beneficial. "All things are lawful," but not all things build up' (1 Cor 10.23).

There can be no drug that is not licit, although there may be many drugs of which we might say they are not recommended. Conversely, there can be no drug which we are commanded to consume, not even wine at the eucharist. We cannot be commanded to consume a drug because, as Paul exhorts us, each should be concerned for the consciences of others in the community, and where patterns of consumption might cause a scandal to 'weaker' members, these substances should be avoided. Thus, for example, the practice of teetotalism by some Baptists in Russia may well be an appropriate response to extremely high rates of alcoholism in that country. But such abstention is a tactical measure, limited by particular circumstances. Nevertheless, our situation is a bit more complex than simply counselling moderation in all things and restraint where appropriate.

If the location of idolatry in a technocratic and consumer culture is the body itself, then there is a direct rivalry between the body as a temple of consumerism and the body as a temple of the Holy Spirit (1 Cor 6.19). If drugs are a primary means of habituating ourselves to a technocratic and consumerist vision of life, then all forms of drug use, therapeutic or otherwise, may be instances of what Paul calls sins against the body. Drug use directly turns the body away from glorifying God and denies that our bodies were 'purchased at a price' through Christ's death and resurrection. Thus, within a technocratic and consumer society, drugs use may turn the body itself (as distinct from the act or substance) into a witness against God in a manner parallel to fornication (1 Cor 6.18). So while we may, in theory, moderately or occasionally consume drugs such as alcohol or tobacco (or even barbiturates and amphetamines), in good conscience, when we recognize how consuming these drugs constitutes a way in which we participate in contemporary forms of idolatry, and how such use makes of our bodies objects of manipulation and consumption by an all pervasive system of domination, then temperance may, in practice, not always be enough. At the present time and in certain circumstances, abstinence may well be a necessary form of gospel witness.

Drug Use in the Redemption and Fulfilment of All Things

As well as being circumscribed by the conditions of witness, all use of drugs is relativized by the gift of the Holy Spirit and the fulfilment of time when there will be no more tears (and thus no more need for therapeutic drugs) and when we shall all be caught up in the euphoric ecstasy of the messianic banquet (and therefore there will be no more unfulfilled desire for personal ecstasy that drugs may simulate and parody).

All drug use is relativized as an activity limited to this age, with no significance in the new creation. Furthermore, we live betwixt this age and the age to come. Any attempt falsely to resolve that tension, either by engineering a permanent contentment now (through 'cosmetic pharmacology') or by chemically induced attempts to experience God's kingdom come, are both ruled out, for they both seek to deny the eschaton as a gift given by God (which may, through the Spirit, be experienced now). We cannot, as Aldous Huxley supposed, use drugs to 'cleanse the doors of perception.' In his influential book detailing his experiences of taking mescaline, Huxley writes that LSD and other such drugs can enable us to see 'what Adam had seen on the morning of his creation—the miracle, moment by moment, of naked existence.'[43] In effect, Huxley makes chemicals rather then Christ the mediator and healer of true perception. But there can be no return to Eden. Drugs cannot directly enable us to see ourselves more clearly, 'for now we see in a mirror, dimly' (1 Cor 13.12). What clarity of vision we can receive is not given by chemicals but by the Holy Spirit, and is an eschatological vision, not a pharmacological one. We cannot use drugs to create what is, in effect, an artificial paradise. The wine of the eucharist is but a provisional supplement to the wine of the Spirit.

We cannot use drugs to create an artifical paradise

As a provisional supplement to the wine of the Spirit, drugs may be used both therapeutically and in an ampliative way to enable personal presence, either through healing the body, or enhancing personal relations. The use of alcohol to promote conviviality is good in the light of the *telos* of human being as communion with God and each other.[44] Indeed, the use of wine to foreshadow the messianic banquet lies at the heart of Jesus' actions at the wedding feast at Cana (John 2.1–11). Conversely, when drugs militate against greater personal presence, and a deepening of communal relations, then a line has been crossed between proper use and abuse. The line between the use of alcohol (or cannabis) to enable conviviality and being drunk (or stoned) is drawn at the point at which alienation and the sundering of personal relations sets in. We must always ask, when someone is using alcohol (or cannabis), whether that person is more or less physically, spiritually, emotionally and rationally present to others, and if they are, at what point does the drug in use inhibit both an individual's present ability, and their future capacity, for personal presence to God and others.[45]

Drugs that create a false, chemically induced sense of profound community (as distinct from a convivial or congenial one) are rendered illicit. While we may anticipate the messianic banquet in this age, such anticipations are shaped by Christ's crucifixion. Our joy in the communion presently available is found as, by the Spirit, we 'put to death the deeds of the body' (Rom 8.13).

The intrinsically strong effect of drugs like ecstasy short-circuits the cruciform nature of personal relations by attempting a technological solution to the painful, time-intensive dynamics of repentance, forgiveness, attentiveness to one's neighbour, sacrificial self-giving, and all the other aspects of personal transformation that are required for profound community between humans.[46] The ecstatic joy of the Prodigal's embrace by his father is entirely different in kind to the unity enjoyed solely under the influence of drugs, the value of which is debased precisely because it is fabricated. One is an event of hard won communion, the other is simply another consumer event. Indeed, rather than bear witness to the life, death and resurrection of Jesus Christ in its life together, such drug-induced patterns of ecstasy and community constitute a parody of it.

A Question of Discernment

What I have said regarding a Christian response to contemporary patterns of drug use can be summarized in the following five tests or questions to address to any form of drug use—ampliative or therapeutic. These questions are designed to consider any drug in the light of the whole of salvation history so as to excavate all its dimensions.

Creation
1   Is the drug being used to manipulate or control the body in a way that denies the body's created goodness and its created limits?

Fall
2   Is the use of the drug idolatrous or not? In a way analogous to meat sacrificed to idols (1 Corinthians) by discerning when, where and how a particular drug is used we can discern whether its use is idolatrous or not.

3   In relation to any particular circumstances or context, is temperance or abstinence called for?

Redemption
4   When someone is using a drug does it make that person more or less physically, spiritually, emotionally and rationally present to others, and if it does, at what point does the drug in use inhibit both an individual's immediate ability and their future capacity for personal presence to God and others?[47]

5   Does the drug used allow for the cruciform shape of redeemed human relations before Christ's return or does it seek to create an artificial paradise?

6   The Churches and Drug Use

To try and identify a single project that deals with this issue in a way that is paradigmatic for the churches is unwise because to do so would immediately mis-locate the 'problem' in one particular section of society. There are many good projects helping those whose lives have been destroyed by dependency on drugs. However, such projects need to be seen within the wider context of the church's mission. The primary emphasis for Christians needs to be on both congregational witness and the witness of the church as a whole rather than on individual projects addressing particular concerns. However, some of the questions we must address in our congregations are these:

- How do our individual lives and our lives as the body of Christ bear witness to the theological vision of drug use set out above?
- Do we practise temperance—not just in relation to alcohol, but in relation to headache pills and the like?
- Do we establish patterns of life that can take account of and involve suffering rather than seek to avoid suffering at all costs or frame it in wholly negative terms?
- When we gather together socially, what is the character of our celebration and how do our parties enable us to be more personally present to each other?
- Is our worship open to ecstatic encounter with God or is it so dull it casts a false glow upon our contemporary religious surrogates such as ecstasy, alcohol or LSD?

These are the kinds of questions we must ask of our church practices. And in doing so, we may become the kinds of communities who can point a way forward to patterns of life that are not drug dependent in the way that most of modern life is. Instead, we will be affirming the reality of the body as a gift of God—subject to sin, but redeemed through the life, death and resurrection of Jesus Christ and open to fulfilment through the perfecting and empowering presence of the Spirit as we await Christ's return.

These are the kinds of questions we must ask of our church practices

Notes

1 For an overview of the inter-relationship between drugs smuggling and terrorism, see J Cooley, *Unholy Wars: Afghanistan, America and International Terrorism* (London: Virginia, 1999) ch 7.

2 See D T Courtwright, *Forces of Habit: Drugs and the Making of the Modern World* (Cambridge, MA: Harvard University Press, 2001) pp 61–64.

3 For a broad ranging discussion of the inter-relationship between all these elements see Courtwright, *Forces of Habit*.

4 Rudi Matthee notes that tobacco, coffee, cocoa, tea and distilled alcohols were introduced at a remarkably similar time and in a uniform way. Tobacco began to be used in Europe from the 1500s onwards, the first distillery was established in 1575 in Holland, coffee was introduced in the early 1600s (the first European coffee house opened in Venice in 1645), as was tea. R Matthee, 'Exotic Substances: the Introduction and Global Spread of Tobacco, Coffee, Cocoa, Tea, and Distilled Liquour, Sixteenth to Eighteenth Centuries,' in R Porter and M Teich (eds), *Drugs and Narcotics in History* (Cambridge: Cambridge University Press, 1995) pp 25–28.

5 On this see the extensive discussion of cannabis throughout R Davenport-Himes, *The Pursuit of Oblivion: A Social History of Drugs* (London: Phoenix Press, 2001).

6 Davenport-Himes, *The Pursuit of Oblivion*, pp 94–96.

7 P Matthews, *Cannabis Culture: A Journey Through Disputed Territory* (London: Bloomsbury, 1999) pp 172–73.

8 Advertisement in the *Illustrated London News* quoted in Matthews, *Cannabis Culture*, p 173.

9 America was very active and influential in promoting prohibitionist policies.

10 For example, Marek Kohn gives an account of how women and racial minorities who used drugs, notably cocaine and opium, became scapegoats for wider social anxieties in Britain in the early twentieth century. M Kohn, *Dope Girls: The Birth of the British Drug Underground* (London: Granta, 1992).

11 Coffee was controversial when it first appeared in the Muslim world in the sixteenth and seventeenth centuries and Charles II tried to suppress coffee houses which were viewed as 'nurseries of idleness' and hotbeds of sedition. Matthee, 'Exotic Substances,' p 36.

12 Matthee, 'Exotic Substances,' p 35.

13 For an overview of the history of the 'war on drugs' (from the late 1960s, when President Nixon coined the phrase 'war on drugs,' to the late 1990s) see

Davenport-Himes, *The Pursuit of Oblivion*, pp 338–83.

14 Strictly speaking, this definition excludes antibiotics, antivirals and preventative medicines such as vaccines since these act on parasites or alien elements in the body as opposed to acting on the body as such.

15 Put simplistically, most ampliative drug use draws on one or more of five types of drugs: *narcotics* (which relieve pain and induce feelings of euphoria: *eg*, opium and its derivatives); *hypnotics* (which cause sleep and can reduce feelings of anxiety: *eg*, sulphonal, and barbiturates); *stimulants* (which cause feelings of excitement and increase mental and physical energy: *eg*, caffeine, tobacco, betal, tea, coca and qat); *inebriants* (which induce drunkenness: *eg*, alcohol, ether, and solvents); *hallucinogens* (which cause complex changes in visual, auditory and other perceptions, *eg*, cannabis, LSD, certain mushrooms, and mescaline). All of them may create dependency, while hallucinogens and stimulants may cause psychotic disturbances. Davenport-Himes, *The Pursuit of Oblivion*, pp ix–x. It should be noted that the above descriptions are *extremely* simplified accounts of what are complex phenomena and many of these classes overlap. At the same time, variations between different drugs must be accounted for.

16 At the heart of this self-contradiction lies the 'modern' conception of freedom. Oliver O'Donovan states: 'Technology derives its social significance from the fact that by it man has discovered new freedoms from necessity. The technological transformation of the modern age has gone hand in hand with the social and political quest of Western man to free himself from the necessities imposed upon him by religion, society and nature. Without this social quest the development of technology would have been unthinkable; without technology the liberal society as we know it would be unworkable.' O O'Donovan, *Begotten or Made?* (Oxford: Clarendon Press, 1984) p 6.

17 P Kramer, *Listening to Prozac* (London: Fourth Estate, 1994).

18 See I Illich, *Limits to Medicine—Medical Nemesis: The Expropriation of Health* (Harmondsworth, Middlesex: Pelican, 1977).

19 C Elliott, *Better Than Well: American Medicine Meets the American Dream* (New York: W W Norton & Co, 2003).

20 Illich, *Limits to Medicine*, p 142.

21 Reflecting on the reasons he used drugs, the writer Will Self articulates exactly these sentiments, stating: 'I revered drug-taking as a blow against conformity and a blow against the hierarchy and a blow against what was quite a privileged middle-class background.' W Self and S Turner, 'Getting a Fix: Steve Turner talks to Will Self,' *Third Way*, 24.5, 2001, p 20.

22 For a wide ranging critique of the use of enhancement technologies in order to be more fulfilled, authentic and psychologically healthier see C Elliot, *Better Than Well*.

23 Z Bauman, *Work, Consumerism and the New Poor* (Buckingham: Open University Press, 1998) p 24.

24 Bauman, *Work, Consumerism and the New Poor*, p 24.

25 R Bocock, *Consumption* (London: Routledge, 1993) p 69.

26 *ibid.*

27 Quoted from Bauman, *Work, Consumerism and the New Poor,* p 28.

28 Bauman states: 'Consumer goods are meant to be used up and to disappear; the idea of temporariness and transitoriness is intrinsic to their very denomination as objects of consumption; consumer goods have *memento mori* written all over them, even if with an invisible ink.' Bauman, *Work, Consumerism and the New Poor,* p 28.

29 In 1999 the US Food and Drug Administration approved Paxil, which, like Prozac, is a selective serotonin reuptake inhibitor. Paxil is designed for use in relation to 'social phobia' or 'social anxiety disorder,' which some suggest are simply technical sounding terms for shyness. GlaxoSmithKline who produce the drug spent $91.8 million advertising Paxil directly to consumers. Elliott, *Better Than Well*, pp 57–9.

30 For a case study of the inter-connection between consumerism, industrialisation, and a technocratic society see the analysis of the emergence of the cigarette industry in Courtwright, *Forces of Habit*, pp 112–132.

31 K Barth, *Church Dogmatics*, III: 4, translated by A T Mackay and others (Edinburgh: T&T Clark, 1961) p 342.

32 *ibid.*

33 Whether it is the chemical effect of a drug that induces a physiological dependency or whether dependency is caused by the fear and pain of withdrawal is a matter of some dispute. A related issue is the interaction between the user's expectation ('set') and their physical and social context ('setting') in determining the effects of drugs. Variables in either of these change the experienced impact of a drug upon the body.

34 There is much debate between those who think drugs can artificially induce dependency in anyone (thus restricting exposure is key) and those who think that the chemicals themselves and their supply matters less than the personal and cultural values that modulate the demand for and use of any particular drug. Proponents of the former view point to the link between proximity and high rates of dependency. Proponents of the latter view point to examples such as the contrast between rates of alcoholism in Ireland and Italy or Spain: despite high levels of *per capita* consumption of alcohol in all these countries alcoholism in Ireland is far more widespread. For an example of the second view see Stanton Peele, 'A Moral Vision of Addiction: How People's Values Determine Whether They Become and Remain Addicts' *Journal of Drug Issues*, 17.2 (1987) pp 187–215.

35 E Brecher, *Licit and Illicit Drugs; the Consumers Union Report on Narcotics, Stimulants, Depressants, Inhalants, Hallucinogens, and Marijuana—Including Caffeine, Nicotine, and Alcohol* (Boston: Little Brown, 1972) ch 5.

36 See R Holmes, *Coleridge: Darker Reflections* (London: Flamingo, 1999).

37 'Temperance,' *New Shorter Oxford English Dictionary*, CD-ROM edition (Oxford: Oxford University Press, 1996).

38 John Paul II, *The Theology of the Body: Human Love in the Divine Plan* (Boston: Pauline Books & Media, 1997) pp 200–201.

39 O O'Donovan, *Resurrection and Moral Order* (Grand Rapids, MI: Eerdmans, 1986) p 12.

40 John Paul II, *The Theology of the Body*, p 205.

41 N T Wright, 'Monotheism, Christology and Ethics: 1 Corinthians 8,' in *The Climax of the Covenant: Christ and the Law in Pauline Theology* (Minneapolis: Fortress Press, 1992) p 125.

42 *ibid*, p 134.

43 *The Doors of Perception and Heaven and Hell* (London: Flamingo, 1994) p 7.

44 It is a false view of human relations to think it is possible to be wholly personally present to everyone all the time. Human relationships properly operate on a scale from casual exchanges in a bus queue to the profound conversations of deep friendship or the vulnerability of sexual intercourse. Conviviality lies somewhere between these two poles.

45 This, of course, raises the huge question of what it means to be personally present to others. Two important and related questions are whether enhancement technologies like Prozac enable or disable authentic personal presence and how such technologies may function to enable the kinds of personal transformation that formation into the form of Christ entails. Discernment of how different drugs affect human relationships and personhood will become ever more pressing with increasing use of psychopharmacology. For a non-theological assessment of the issues see C Elliott, *Better Than Well*.

46 However, this is not to rule out the possibility that milder forms that have an effect analogous to small quantities of alcohol may be licit.

47 An obvious boundary case is the use of opiates in palliative care.